"Daddy, Where Are You?"
MIA or POW?

by

Brenda Miller

"Daddy, Where Are You?"
MIA or POW?

Brenda Miller

ISBN: 979-8-9918386-6-5

Library of Congress Control Number: 2025905324

Published and Printed in the United States of America

Brenda Miller, *"Daddy, Where Are You? MIA or POW?"*

Copyright © 2025 by Brenda Miller

Publisher: G Publishing LLC

Editor: Anthony Ambrogio

Cover Design by SOS Graphic Design

Dedication

To the Lord Jesus Christ and the Holy Spirit, who continually reminded me I was to write a book.

To the parents and students of Southfield-Lathrup High School, who trusted me with their dilemmas and personal worries. It is because of you that I began writing this book 12 years ago.

To my children and grandchildren....I love you and I pray you are proud of me.

With all else said, to God be the glory, forever and ever. Amen

Acknowledgements

No one could have told me about 20 or more years ago that I was going to write a book. When God sends a word to you, He has already placed in you what is needed to get the task done, but it took me a while to see myself in that light.

- Minister Barbara Davis and Pastor Donna Fox, my girlfriends since 1980 or so, thank you for speaking a word in season and out.

I want to also acknowledge the following people who over the years of my walk with God from the very beginning until now and because of their ministry and gifting have played an intricate part in my life:

- Pastor Leon Glover (deceased), Acts Full Gospel Church, Detroit, MI. *He would always motivate me by calling me, "Preacher/Teacher"*

- Bishop Corletta J. Vaughn, Holy Ghost Cathedral, Detroit, MI. *Thank you for the word from God to ignite the writing and the love you have given me. I truly love you, and I am so glad God connected us. You help bring out the best in me. Love you to the moon!*

- Apostle Calvern Woods, Charis Cathedral, Pittsburgh, PA. *Thank you for showing me God has a sense of humor. I understood revelation of the word through your preaching. Love you!*

- Dr. Grace Moorman (deceased), Amazing Grace of God Ministry, Detroit, MI. *Dr. Moorman was an excellent teacher, advocate, and "girlie friend." She is truly missed.*

- Apostle Velma Clopton, Glory House International Church, Mesa, AZ. *Thank you, Woman of God, for igniting the prophetic gift in me and teaching me all things pertaining to my gift*

- Bishop Willie Thornton, King of Kings International Church, Wayne, MI. *The first time I met you, you asked if you knew me. Other questions led to "Well, I know you in the spirit." From then on, we formed a friendship. Thank you for your grace and love.*

- My pastors, Apostle Joseph and Pastor Brenda Hobbs, Triumphant Life Christian Church in Highland Park, MI. *Thank you so much for your encouragement and love. You are truly a man and woman after God's own heart.*

- My Remnant sisters—Apostle Alta Davis, Apostle Karen Bruce, Prophet LaVondia Eldridge, Prophet Debrah Chavis, and Pastor Angela Watkins—who always keep me in prayer and speak into my life. *I love you ladies so much! God hand-picked us to be remnant sisters.*

Table of Contents

Foreword

I've been told for many years now that I must write, but I was always asking myself, "Write what?" I did do a little journaling from time to time when I felt I had something to say. It wasn't that I didn't have anything to say; it's just that got tired of writing (fingers get tired, you know), and I was always trying to find one of those beautiful journals that someone had given me for a present. How many of you know that God doesn't change His mind as to what He has called you to do? Right! So, He hasn't changed his mind on me writing and for that matter going to school. LOL! That's coming in the fall.

Two things happened to me that made me take writing so seriously:

1. I was at Holy Ghost Cathedral on December 30, 2012 to be anointed by Apostle Corletta Vaughn. She was

hosting a Pre-Watchnight service. She had just returned from Israel and brought back some anointing oil. I knew in my spirit I had to be there to get anointed for the New Year by this mighty woman of God whom I love. Now, mind you, she had no idea what had been prophesied (spoken) over my life previously to my arrival there. The first thing she said to me was, "Miller, you got to write!" This messed me up! *What?* She said, "There are annals in you; the power is not in your preaching but in the book," and opened up her hands like a book. "There is fire there." Need I say more? It messed me up!

2. I had lunch with my niece Heather (aka Shellie), and I was just talking—about nothing special, I thought—but she found it to be so. She said, "Auntie, this is a

book." *Huh! Not you, too?* LOL! So she and I finally met to find out where she was coming from about this book. Everything has been clarified, and so here I am.

This book consists of true stories and issues that I have dealt with since I have worked in the public-school system. Names have been changed, but the stories are real.

I began working in the school system in September 1996. It was a break from my 20-year stint working for the federal government. A parent that I knew asked if I would mind working along with her at one of the schools as a Noon Aide, and, as they say, the rest is history.

This was a new line of work for me, and it blew my mind! In the lunchroom it's so loud that you want to tell all the students to be quiet, but I was informed I would get used to it and that this was the place where they were able to release some energy. Well, the part about the noise was true: in about two-three weeks, it didn't bother me. The thing that did bother me was the behavior of some of the students. Mind you, this was a middle school, and seeing 11- to 13-year-old students behave badly brought out my motherly instincts but always from a place of love.

The experience also gave me a chance to see what the teachers learn in college about development levels and what most children do at the different ages: I was learning as I was working. During that time, I got to know a couple of sons and about four daughters. They left and went on to high school, and neither I nor they imagined that I would see them in high school.

After working in the middle school for four years, I wanted more hours, but the only way I could get them was to apply and test for a substitute-secretary position within the district.

Which I did. After 1½ years, I applied for a permanent full-time-secretary position and received it.

On August 9, 2001, I began my high-school position. *Woooweee*, nobody could tell me it would be like this. Children acted like they were just hatched and not raised. Wild and free….hmm.

Ah, the high school age—14-18 years old. My God, can't tell them nothing! I believe they say to themselves, "We have arrived," not knowing they still have rules and policies to adhere to. This is the "hot-mess" stage. They labeled me the "mean lady" because I would only let them be children and not think they were adults, but, as they began to get to know me, they found out I'm really a softy as long as you behave yourself.

I also learned that this generation of children was very verbal. It was not like it was when I was growing up. When an adult was talking to you,

you were to keep quiet, and, if you spoke out of turn, you got … well, you know. I grew to understand this generation's behavior in that regard, and, so, while I maintained a standard which I was not going to change, I allowed them to be verbal but with respect. If they couldn't pull it together, I put them out of my office. Oh, they could come back, but they must remember the rules of my office.

I found that this generation really would try and manipulate you, lie to you (this is an understatement), and downright not care what you thought or said (because "It's all about me!"), but, despite it all, I must say I have found pleasure in the students and have been glad that I was able to help them become their better selves by listening, letting them cry, or giving a hug. These 14- to 18-year-olds have a lot that they must deal with: peer pressure, self-esteem issues, home life, etc. The biggest thing is home life.

Some parents need to attend a Parenting University!

Too many parents (especially moms) want to be their children's friends. **NO, NO! This is not an option. That line is too thin, don't cross it!** Trust me; I caught it from my daughter during that time because she wanted me to be friends with her like some of her girlfriends were with their moms. I couldn't do it because, when I needed to be the mom, that's when rebellion would set in and my daughter would complain, "My girlfriends don't talk to me like that and don't tell ME what to do!" Too bad; I am not your friend; I am your *mother*. Moms catch the hell and receive the respect. Your children will thank you for your discipline and guidance later. My daughter finally got it. *WHEW!*

Pray, moms…that's what we are suppose to do, and I prayed like crazy because I was going to either take my kid to a youth home or hurt her really bad! CAN SOMEBODY SAY, "BUT GOD!" YES SIR!

Now, dads, this goes for you too! I know oh so well about daddy's little angel. Come on now; you gotta help the moms out! We need you to discipline too and have our backs. Those of you, who no longer live in the home, put away the differences that you may have against your ex and vice versa and come together to help raise these children. You weren't fussing and bickering when you made them.

With all that said, I pray that this book will bless you in every aspect of your life and in your children as you bring forth change in your home, your children's lives, and your spiritual life.

Be Blessed.

Tuesday, July 30, 2013

Chapter 1: The Beginning

"Well, when tackling a tall piece of cheese, start at the beginning," says Father Mouse in the Christmas cartoon *'Twas the Night Before Christmas*. I have completed 12 years as a high-school secretary, and, as I start every new school year, I try to do something to make my work—or should I say work *life*—a little easier. I'm the school's bookkeeper, and bookkeeping is where all of my adventures take place. Trying to collect money from people with financial obligations is a chore to say the least, but I do my job, and, I must say, I do it well.

My first year retrieving payment from students and parents was a mind opener. One incident involved a check that a student had written to pay for his financial obligation; the check was returned. I called the student's home (he was a senior at the time), and the mom went off, telling me, "He's 18 years old and grown, and I'm not paying anything." WOW! The parent didn't make her son have any accountability for bouncing a check.

Well, whatever the parents don't do, the world surely will. Trust me—you would rather have your parents do it instead of the world because the world has no love.

This parent wasn't the only one to take that "I'm not gonna pay" attitude. So, after my administrator and I talked, we decided that no personal checks would be taken for any financial obligations. Cash, money orders, and cashier checks only! A lot of parents were not happy, but that's what happens when, as the old saying goes, "One bad apple spoils the whole bunch."

As the years went on there was always some issue about students and parents and paying. I'll never forget this incident. Two students had a financial obligation and decided they weren't going to pay because—well—they just weren't going to pay despite the fact that they had used the services, gone on the trips, and done everything else. I had to put my mama hat and voice on. I let them know that they were not going to "pimp" this teacher and they WOULD pay. I let them know that their manipulation and cheating was unacceptable and they would "reap that which they have sown." One student said, "Yes ma'am, yes ma'am," and pulled the money out of his pocket. The other one got mad and left, but, before he left, I let him know that I didn't care. He should have thought about his actions before he did them. He finally did take care of his obligation. To say the least, that student stopped his scandalous ways, and I must say he has turned out to be a great person.

As the years went by, I remember cap-and-gown pick-up for the seniors, which meant they had to pay their obligation first before they could pick up their cap and gown. I must say it was a stressful time, but I tried to have fun with it. It was like I was off to the races; the list had been posted, and it was time to let the seniors in. I had books that were returned and books that had to be paid for. To relieve the stress, I turned on my music. I had some "old school" rocking, and the students were loving it.

Once the students got to see me in action and knew I was just doing my job, they offered to go to the store for me and bring me water or a pop. With the students observing me in action (smile), they found that they could get more flies with honey than with vinegar, so, even if they were wrong, they allowed the honey to flow!

I still had some students who thought they could talk to me any way they wanted, but shortly they were reminded where they were at. One student got so nasty with me I put him out, and he brought his mom back up to the school. After she and I had a conversation, he had to pay out of his funds, which he didn't like. His mom asked what she could do for me (really for him); I asked for some food because I hadn't eaten lunch, and they went and bought my lunch.

I remember one student who came into my office and said, "Mrs. Miller, I'm not going to give you a hard time, so just take ALL my little money, but, if somebody else turns in my book, will you call me, and can I get my money back?" I told him no problem but it was his demeanor that I loved because he had me laughing even though I was so tired and I felt like crying. That one student made it all good for me, and, when I see him, I always remind him of that. Of course, he has done well. He finished his undergrad at Michigan State and, I believe, his master's at the University of Michigan.

Oh, I forgot to tell you that I work on senior fines from 1:00-4:30 p.m. non-stop, *whew!*

Now, parents, when you don't pay, if you bounce checks and try and manipulate the system, that is just wrong! You send the wrong message to your children because, if we, as parents, really look at it, we are our children's biggest role models. Not the rappers, sports figures, or aunts and uncles. Our children see us every day. They mimic us and see the good, the bad, and the ugly in us, but they still want to be like us and not "like Mike." \

I've had parents come and try to bully me, threaten me, and whatever else. To those parents, I stand my ground. Now, I have parents who know how to talk to me (here's the honey), and with them I use my compassion and the little bit of authority I have as a bookkeeper to accommodate them.

I must tell you I have been taken for a ride! I was too thorough! I had a dad whose student was leaving the school district, but the student had some outstanding financial obligations. Remember that I told you earlier that I didn't take personal checks! Well, this dad (don't get it twisted; he wasn't fine) really almost begged me to take his check, and his reasoning was good, but I kept saying to him, "Sir, don't burn me!" Well, he burned me for a nice sum. That joker had closed that checking account, and need I say that for two years after that everybody else paid the price. NO PERSONAL CHECKS AND NO EXCUSES!

When I speak about bullying, I had a parent who had two students at the school, who both had outstanding fines. I was sitting at my desk, and the mom and her students were standing in front of me. This parent and I had had conversations before about various things because one of her students always had some sort of fine. As we were talking, her student starting say, "Come on, mama; we ain't gotta listen to her; she ain't nobody!" Well, to say the least when I got finished with that student and his mom, the other student didn't stay around to get theirs. All three of them tried to gang up on me, and, if you know me, **that is not happening.**

When the administrator came and I had to explain what happened, the mother tried to say it was my fault and I really didn't have to say what I said, but at no time did she correct her student not to talk to me in that matter. He needed to be mine!

I must tell you, I really felt bad because there were other parents waiting to be taken care of, and I felt I had to show out instead of being professional. I did apologize to the parents, who told me they understood and accepted my apology. One male parent even said he was getting ready to come to my desk to help me out! There are parents still out there whose beliefs are like yours!

Parents, let's teach our children to respect everyone, including students who are their same age but especially their elders (adults). The bible tells us to, "Train up a child in the way he should go: and when he is old, he will not depart from it." (Proverbs 22:6, KJV). Also, parents, we must let our children know that the word of God tells them as children, "Honor your father and mother"—which is the first commandment with a promise—"that it may go well with you and that you may enjoy long life on the earth." (Eph 6:2-3, NIV).

I don't know what has happened to some parents. I mean, was your upbringing so bad that you threw the baby out with the bathwater, or were you a baby having a baby and now you just want to live your life? Maybe because you didn't have the help of the father in raising your child, you just gave up.

I truly believe that, if it's not broke, don't try to fix it. That's when everything just goes haywire. So don't give up and don't throw in the towel, God's got your back, and He can give you the strength and wisdom you need to endure until your change comes.

One last thing, in my life time I have found Ephesians 6:2-3 to be true. I remember some years ago—maybe in the '80s—that a mom was getting ready to go to the store. Her son was down the street hanging out with some of the neighborhood boys (a group she didn't like him spending so much time with), so she called him home and told him to stay in the house until she got back. She reiterated to him before leaving, "DO NOT LEAVE THIS HOUSE AND GO BACK DOWN THE STREET." Well, he was "hardheaded," as my generation would say, and he went back to hang out with the boys.

When the mom returned from the store, she noticed a lot of police cars on her street and near her house. The neighbors were out; it was just chaos. When she asked what was going on, she was taken to the side by the police and told that her son was dead. He had been shot in the head because one of the boys had a gun and was playing "Russian Roulette." I can only imagine how that mom felt. She had only been gone about 45 minutes to an hour. We must teach our children how to be obedient and respectful so that they will have long life on this earth. I have never forgotten that incident because it proved for me that the word of God is true.

Chapter 2: Parents...."Now Hear This"

Being a parent is hard—especially if you are a single parent. As parents, we must work, monitor our children, pay bills, find time (quality time) to spend with our children, our spouse, and ourselves. Our jobs are demanding and sometimes cause us to think the job is more important than our family, but that is so far from the truth. It's true we need our jobs to pay the bills and car notes, buy clothes, buy food, etc., but one thing that we have to realize as parents is that we are here on this Earth for one season, and, when that season is over, we are gone. And, when we leave this side of terra firma, we leave the job, friends, and, most importantly, our family. So, really, who's the most important?

I believe that we lose perspective when it comes to the importance of our jobs over our families. As I said, when we leave this Earth, our families will be the most affected by our absence. As for the job, our employers will quickly replace us, although, for a brief, very brief moment, they may talk about how good or not so good we were. During that time, our family will be grieving, wondering how they are going to make it without us.

For some people, it takes a life time to get over a loss. With others, we learn to move on, but, in certain special moments or when we're just sitting back thinking about the family member no longer with us, our emotions overwhelm us. Sometimes we think about the things we could have or should have done and said or how we could have done something special for them or not given them any problems. Also, some of us forget to tell them that we love them.

I've written all of this in order to say, "FIND TIME TO SPEND WITH YOUR CHILDREN AND TO SPEND TIME AS A FAMILY."

Never forget to tell them you LOVE them. Hug and kiss them like it's the last time you will see them. Life is too short, and tomorrow is not promised to us. Live for the day and don't procrastinate about tomorrow because, before you know it, today is gone and tomorrow is too! "So don't be anxious about tomorrow. God will take care of your tomorrow too. Live one day at a time." (Matt 6:34, TLB)

To single moms and dads, you have it especially hard because the other parent may only help, spend time, or have visitation rights every so often, which leaves you to be everything. For you, it causes anguish, anger, and physical and mental stress. Trying to be everything to everybody and do everything is a feat in itself, which most times sets us up for failure to ourselves and our family. We don't have an "S" on our chest or walk around with superhuman powers; we fail emotionally and sometimes physically, so we need to understand and remember that we are only human and can only do so much in one day.

Whatever you cannot do, try and incorporate some help from other parents, friends that you trust, or your own parents. It's been said that exercise, yoga, meditation, or walking can release endorphins that will relax you and bring you peace. All the above are great, but my greatest release is meditation and prayer to God our Father. He can bring comfort, peace, and understanding. He'll give you wisdom and remove all doubts. You can talk to Him about anything that's going on in your world and He will give you the answers.

- "Trust in the Lord with all your heart and lean not on your own understanding; in all your ways acknowledge him, and he will make your paths straight." (Prov 3:5-6, NIV)

- "Do not be anxious about anything, but in everything, by prayer and petition, with thanksgiving, present your requests to God. And the peace of God, which transcends all understanding, will guard your hearts and your minds in Christ Jesus." (Phil 4:6-7, NIV)

- "I cannot do everything so I choose those things which are vital and excellent and of real value. I have wisdom and I am able to distinguish the highest and the best things for me to do." (Phil 1:10, AMP)

- "Good sense makes me restrain my anger, and it is my glory to overlook a transgression or an offense." (Prov 19:11, AMP)

I have written all of this is because of my encounters with students. They tell me about how their moms (usually in a single-parent home) don't have time or don't spend time with them. The time that mom thinks they want is going shopping (which is okay), but, really, they just want some sit-down time at a restaurant, a park, or even at home watching a movie together and talking about their stresses of the day. They need you as a parent to give some answers and wisdom to help them out. These are the special times, the great times. Not only that, they help you as a parent to really get to know your child. We think we know them, but sometimes we really don't. This generation of children come up against so many things and pressures that the world and their peers throw at them.

As parents, we also tend to believe everything our child tells us because they know how to really work us over. Manipulation is the game played because they know us better than we know them. Trust me; my son got me for about a year regarding his degree from Oakland University. He told me everything under the sun, and I believed him. He knew me better than I thought. My daughter kept telling me that he was lying to me because she had already received her undergrad degree and was working on her masters. Finally, things started not adding up, and I had to go into psycho-mom mode to get him to tell me the truth. So, to say the least, he had no choice but to go back to school (4-1/2 years) and take the one class (0.5 credit) he needed to receive his degree, which I have at my house.

Mom and dad, investigate things—especially if they sound too good to be true. You'll be surprised! I also believe in the scripture, "Train up a child in which way they should go, and they will not depart from it" (Proverbs 22:6)—but wisdom has led me to believe that, when we do this, they still have their own mind and, for whatever reason, will do what they want (my son did). But the good thing is that, with continued prayer on your part, they do come back to those things which you have instilled in them.

Don't beat up yourself and please, please, don't yell back at them, "I raised you better than that!" because you did—but they chose to do their own thing. Sometimes life excites them, and they feel that parents are just being overly rigid, so they step out into the excitement only to find everything that looks good is not good. You must be there to give them the comfort they need, help them to get back on track, and sometimes let them know there will be consequences for their actions.

I remember when Bishop Corletta Vaughn told our class one day that, since we'd gotten older, we'd forgotten some of the things we did growing up, and—you know what?—sometimes sharing those things with our children makes us more real and not stuffy. Use wisdom when sharing and decide how much to share. I've shared my youth with both of my children, but more with my daughter because of the things that we as women go through; we can't be afraid to share or think that our children will think badly of us. Know your child and assess the situation.

Sometimes, relating your past experiences will free you for today and your future. So keep on praying and asking God for wisdom for every circumstance in your and your child's life.

- "I always pray, I don't faint, quit or give up." (Luke 18:1, AMP)

- "I will be unceasing in prayer [praying perseveringly]." (1 Thess 5:17, AMP)

A Special Note to Moms

We become everything to everybody, and we lose who we are. Before we got married, had children, and got the dream job, there were things that we enjoyed doing, but we got lost in the race called life. Move yourself back from this race by calling a "Mother's Day." No, I'm not talking about the calendar Mother's Day the second Sunday in May. This Mother's Day is whenever you want it. If you are married, talk to your husband and let him know how you feel and ask him to come on board with you. That day, he would be responsible for taking care of the children. If you are single, call your children's dad and ask him to take them for a few hours or overnight. If the dad is not in their lives, then ask a friend or your parents. This is a much-needed time for us as women because, if we don't find time for what we like, we will feel like something is missing within us, and we will never figure it out. We suffer emotionally, which causes physical problems. Don't be caught there.

I'm sharing this with you because there was a time in my life when my children were my world. My world revolved around them. They went everywhere with me, including when I visited my friends. One day, I was hanging out with some friends, and we were talking. Everybody was talking about what they love to do and when they were doing it. Then they asked me what I liked to do, and—you know what?—I couldn't answer the question. The single unmarried me loved to go shopping, read a good book, hang out with friends, and every now and then go partying.

Not being able to answer that question saddened me, and it really caused me to think about my life. My children were about seven and four at the time, so I thought their father could handle them on his own once in a while. I had a conversation with my husband and told him my feelings and said that I was going to have a "Mother's Day" every now and then, but I would let him know at least three days prior to my day.

My very first Mother's Day was on a pay day (Friday). I changed clothes at work because I wore a uniform and headed over to my favorite mall, Fairlane. I had dinner at Ruby Tuesdays, did a little shopping at Hudson's (now Macy's), and stopped by the house of a cousin I had not seen or talked to in ages.

But, you know, as mothers we worry about our children, so I called home (from a landline; there were no cell phones at the time), and my children were crying. I can laugh about it now, but I couldn't then. I was thinking, *What in the world?*

My daughter told me their dad hadn't fed them and they were hungry. She said he was being mean, too! She put her dad on the phone. Want to know his excuse for not feeding them? He "didn't know what to feed them" (really!). I told him to ask them, and they would tell him what they wanted to eat. They ate pizza from Red Devil Pizzeria and were happy.

As time rolled on, I would call Mother's Day at least once every two to three months. This helped me renew who I was, and it helped my husband get to know his children. Now, moms, this is the technological age, so, when you go out, put your phones on vibrate. No texting, no calling home, no looking at web cams that you may have set up in your house! This is your time to relax and enjoy you.

Ladies: Happy Mother's Day! Enjoy because you deserve it!

To Married Dads

I know you are probably saying "What?"—but think about it: you get more free time to do you than the mom does, so this is a golden opportunity for you to bond, share with, and shed some light on your children, letting them know who you are and what you are all about. In other words, let them find out if you are a funny person, if you love sports and which ones, if you played sports in your youth. It gives you a chance to brag on yourself to your children, explain what things you like to do and why, or just to sit down and pick their brains.

Spending "Mother's Day" with your kids is an awesome opportunity for you. You have to remember that time is moving so fast nowadays; before you know it, your children will be graduating from high school, going to college, graduating from college, and then moving out on their own—at which point, all you can say is "Where did the time go?"

Don't let the time pass you by. Live in the day and grab all the good that it has for you. Also, dad, there is something else you can do for mom…give her date night with you so that you and she can spend that needed time together to share and, as the old folks say, "court again."

As we get older, we are evolving. Our ideas change; our likes and dislikes change, so, as partners, we need to keep each other abreast of these things. I can say from experience that what would rock my boat at 40 years old does not faze me at 50+ years old. I'm in a place now where I will let you know what I think about a situation, but I'm not going to go ballistic about it because "if you like it, I love it." I don't have to reap the consequences for the decisions you make, but I'm there for you.

Dads go for it! You'll be better for it.

To Single Dads

Do like the single moms and call a "Father's Day." You are deserving too,! After all, this nurturing thing is new to you. For whatever reason has made you a single dad, you too must take on some characteristics and roles of a mother, and this is where compassion and patience come in. Learning how to dress and comb your daughters' hair, monitoring computer and TV time, cooking, and helping with homework—as well as a lot more things that come with parenting and raising children. So there…enough said. You, too, deserve this time of relaxation and recuperation.

Later in this book, I will give you some excerpts from two books that I read a good while ago. The titles are *Why a Daughter Needs a Mom* and *Why a Daughter Needs a Dad*. These books are a series of writings by Gregory E. Lang, and they are so powerful. In his other writings, he also addresses why a son needs a mother and dad. Get ready because it's going to bless you real good!

Chapter 3: Father/Dad…MIA (Missing in Action) or POW (Prisoner of War)

As I began to delve deeper into writing this book, I began to see it was about not just parenting but about telling my story from my experiences with female students in relation to their emotions when it came to dealing with the pain of dad not being in their lives the way they wanted them to be and with their mom's pain because of what happened to her and dad's relationship (a situation that can lead to discord between mom and daughter).

I was told once that a father is the sperm donor, but a dad is the one that gives his all for you—the one who provides and spends time with you. No matter what the defining term is, dad, we need you. As daughters, you are our hero, our knight in shining armor who will protect and love us, no matter what. Even when you get mad at us, it breaks your heart. You must discipline us, but only because you know that it will make us better. When you discipline us, it breaks our hearts, too, because we feel we have disappointed you. We are "daddy's little girl," and, again, we need you for that manly guidance to keep us on the right track and to help us not to become needy young ladies and women.

The MIA Father/Dad

The MIA father is the father/dad who may live in the area near the daughter or out of the state but who can be found…never—or only every now and then. In other words, they aren't dead (though they might as well be). This person doesn't give of his time or his love, feeling that, because he gives his money (child support), everything is fine. Usually, when this person does contact his daughter, she's so frustrated that there is always an argument, and things are said that hurt both people, so neither then communicates with the other for another long time. Daughter says she hates him or he's not her father/dad. He's saying, "She's not gonna disrespect me!", but what he doesn't realize is he hasn't done anything to receive that respect in her eyes. What he also doesn't understand is that her "disrespect" is her way of crying out to him, saying, "I need you; I love you, and I want you in my life." I've had so many young girls tell me this very thing. When they begin to share with me, their eyes fill up with tears.

*****

Father/dads, you need to let your little girl, young lady, or woman know that you love her with everything that is in you. Don't talk about what your relationship is like with her mother because she truly doesn't want to hear it. Spend time with her, going out to eat (please *talk*), going to the show, the zoo, etc. The mall is too easy and too much of a distraction because you will spend your money on things and never use the time to get to know her. Be ready to answer the "hard questions" and don't lie. Ask God for wisdom on how to respond so that her feelings are not hurt. (The worst thing you can say to her is, "It's none of your business.") Sometimes we must expose ourselves to help our children understand we have been through some things too, and you will be surprised to find out that such admissions will be healing for you. Remember to ask for wisdom from God and to be tactful.

*****

The other thing that breaks their hearts is when father/dad gets remarried and doesn't include them. No, father/dad, they may not live with you, but you must make them feel they are a part of this new **blended family**. When they come and visit for the weekend or weeks, they should have their own space too.

Embrace your daughter and don't make her feel like an outcast, unwanted, or a stepchild. She is just as important as the stepchildren you have inherited.

True story: a dad came in to pay for his daughter's fine because she was leaving the school. He called mom to let her know that she owed money and how much. While he was talking, mom went to another place talking about finances. The look on his face was too funny. When he hung up, he said under his breath that he would just get his money back from the child-support check.

By then I was in full blown laughter. I was trying to be Ms. Intervention and said, "Now, dad, you know you have to take care of her."

"I do," he replied.

I asked, "Do you spend time with her?"

He replied, "I do."

I said, "Good for you."

Then he told me, "I do all of that, but, guess what ,ma'am: I'm the stepfather!"

After that, I totally lost it. I couldn't talk for laughing. I bowed to him telling him what a good man he was. Later I wondered where her biological dad was and if was he spending time with her or just leaving it to the step dad and sending his money.

The POW Father/Dad

The POW father/dad has been living in a war zone called "my ex-wife," "my ex-girlfriend," or "ex-boo"—whatever word you want to use. Every time he tries to see his daughter, there is drama. The ex has on her war clothes, ready to do battle at just a mention of his name. He has become a "prisoner of this war" called fatherhood/parenting.

The pain the mother feels is the pain she's going to have him feeling for the rest of his life.

Oh, Lord. what he did to me! She's not going anywhere with him because he did this, that, or the other to ME. The daughter is caught like a monkey in the middle, reaching out to grab the hand of the father/dad because she so desperately needs him, but she keeps getting pulled back by "drama mama" because the mother can't let go of the past and allow herself to be healed or set free and live again. So she keeps everyone in her prison.

What's a father/dad to do? He begins to text the daughter and even meets up with her without the knowledge of mom. *What a joy!* Then drama mama finds out…. *Oh snap, it's on and popping!*

Now another level of drama ensues until the daughter is screaming her head off, telling drama mama she's going to see her father/dad and doesn't care what her mother says. In fact, better yet, she tells her mom, "I DON'T WANT TO LIVE WITH YOU ANYMORE!" The shock of it all brings drama mama out of her madness, but now, out of hurt, drama mama tells the daughter, "Go ahead, but you'll be back because he's not this or that."

*****

Father/dads, stop being POWs so you can spend drama-free time with your daughter. Whatever happened in your relationship or marriage, your daughter had nothing to do with it. You need to break out of your prison that the mom has placed you in. Go to her and mend the breach that is between the two of you. Listen to her, let her pour her heart out to you and even tell you off, if necessary. Don't tell her she's wrong or you didn't do this or that; just ask her to forgive you and let her know it was never your intention…

And, moms, the same thing goes for you! It takes two to make a marriage (relationship) and two to break one up.

- "Bear with each other and forgive whatever grievances you may have against one another. Forgive as the Lord forgave you." (Col 3:13-14, NIV)

*****

As I close this chapter, I want to tell you that I am a daddy's girl. Everywhere my dad went, I wanted to go. We talked, and, for every question I asked, he had the answer. My daddy was my hero even when he let me down. It was the love for him and from him that never let me stay mad at him for long periods of time.

There was a time in my life, as a little girl, when I thought my daddy could do no wrong and could do everything. I remember when I was five years old—back then, we went to kindergarten for half days, and I went in the morning. Anyway, when my dad got off from work, my mother would say it was time for us to go hide so that he could find us. We would hide, and, when he found me, he would just pick me up and hug me . I then would ask him about his day at work.

My dad was the wisest man that I knew. He had an eleventh-grade education but was smart as a whip and very wise. Well, he's not with me anymore; he died December 27, 2010, and I miss him so much. I miss seeing him, and, when I need wise counsel, he's no longer there.

Father/dad or whatever title you like, time is of the essence, and your daughter needs you now. It's time to get busy mending relationships and annihilating the MIA and POW status. She needs you right now. Hurry up and don't delay.

To the Moms (POW/MIA)

Moms, now is the time to forgive and release the father/dad's from his position as a POW/MIA. Through this forgiveness, you will receive your freedom from the hurt, anger, and downright nastiness of your past relationship.

Now it's your time to be free. You will feel such a heaviness lifting from you, and you will wonder what took you so long. Just think (if your dad is in your life) how would you feel if your father/dad was not a part of your life. What would you have done or how would you have turned out as an adult? Now think about your daughter…! Wouldn't you just love not to bicker and fight all the time with your daughter about her father/dad? I think so because doing that all the time becomes exhausting. Now, I will say this, if there is something going on in the father/dad's life or someone in the father/dad's life that you are not too fond of, talk it out, work it out, even if it means coming up with a mutally agreed-upon place where your daughter and your ex can spend time. It is deliverance time for everyone!

Life Is Short

I always say, "Life is too short for the bull!" Father time's clock is steadily ticking, and now time seems to move so fast that three months ago feels like two weeks ago. We lose precious time when we don't forgive, when we hold on to anger, and don't adopt that "get back spirit." When we truly come to our senses that baby girl has become a young woman who has taken on the baggage of her parents and is now weighed down with it. The baggage she has taken on has multiplied and her unforgiveness and anger has taken on a different set of "get back" rules. She begins to look for love in all the wrong places and doing the wrong things. She also has a false sense of what love from a man really is because she never had her father to show or teach her how a woman should be loved by a man. Let's stop thinking about the past and move on! Live in the now and allow God to heal all of you from the past. The word of God tells us:

- "Do not remember the former things, nor consider the things of old. Behold, I will do a new thing, now it shall spring forth; Shall you not know it?" (Isa. 43:18-19a, NKJV)

- "In your anger do not sin": Do not let the sun go down while you are still angry, and do not give the devil a foothold." (Eph 4:26-27, NIV)

- "Get rid of all bitterness, rage and anger, brawling and slander, along with every form of malice. Be kind and compassionate to one another, forgiving each other, just as in Christ God forgave you." (Eph 4:31-32, NIV)

Listen Up

When all is said and done, what are you going to do? God is about family; He loves the family unit and is creator of the man and women.

Through their union comes the child(ren). Therefore, God hold parents responsible for the upbringing and outcome of their children's lives. Proverbs 22:6 says, "Train up a child in the way he should go: and when he is old, he will not depart from it". (KJV)

Fathers and mothers both have important roles in their children's lives. I will share with you some excerpts from the books of Gregory E. Lang, *Why a Daughter Needs a Mother* and *Why a Daughter Needs a Father*. These excerpts will allow you to see the importance of your roles as parents, whether you are married, divorced, or separated.

Why a Daughter Needs a Dad: 100

Reasons

Gregory E. Lang

- ❖ To learn that when he says it will be okay soon, it will
- ❖ To share in her joys and triumphs as she grows up and grows older
- ❖ To teach her that her value as a person is more than the way she looks
- ❖ To teach her to believe that she deserves to be treated well
- ❖ To teach her to weigh the consequences of her actions and make decisions accordingly
- ❖ To join her journey when she is too afraid to walk alone
- ❖ To teach her that forgiving is a natural thing to do
- ❖ To teach her that she can forgive more than once
- ❖ To be the safe spot she can always turn to
- ❖ To show her how it feels to be loved unselfishly
- ❖ To be the standard against which she will judge all men

- ❖ Who will let her know that while she may not be the center of someone else's world, she is the center of his
- ❖ To hold her as she cries
- ❖ To teach her that a man's strength is not the force of his hand or his voice, but the kindness of his heart
- ❖ To set a moral standard for her
- ❖ To teach her the importance of being a lady
- ❖ To tell her all she needs to know about boys
- ❖ To show her that all boys are not like the one who hurt her
- ❖ To teach her how to recognize a gentleman
- ❖ So she learns that men can be trustworthy
- ❖ To share with her the wisdom she has not yet acquired
- ❖ To pull her back when she is headed in the wrong direction
- ❖ To learn what she should expect from her husband
- ❖ Who will not punish her for her mistakes, but help her learn from them (Lang, 2012)

Why a Daughter Needs a Mom: 100

Reasons

Gregory E. Lang

- ❖ Teach her how to be a lady
- ❖ To soothe the pain of a broken heart
- ❖ To prepare her for what she will face when she leaves home
- ❖ To teach her that sometimes choosing to wait is a good idea
- ❖ To teach her that you cannot make someone love you, but you can be someone who can be loved
- ❖ To tell her what she should expect from a good man
- ❖ To tell her not to let pride get in the way of forgiving someone
- ❖ To encourage her to be grateful
- ❖ To give her the freedom to express herself
- ❖ To listen closely to what troubles her
- ❖ To share in her excitement when she falls in love for the first time
- ❖ To love her for who she is
- ❖ To teach her that her body is a temple
- ❖ To help her distinguish the difference between love and lust
- ❖ To remind her that there is a rainbow after every storm

- ❖ To teach her that she is responsible for her own happiness
- ❖ Who never hesitates to show affection
- ❖ To assure her that she always has a place to come home to
- ❖ To comfort her through her tears
- ❖ Who tells her of the special place she holds in her heart
- ❖ Because without her she will have less in her life than she deserves (Lang, 2006)

As you can see, God is a God of order and design, but we, as His children, must get in line, fall in line, or do whatever to make certain our children are raised correctly. Are we perfect? No, but we should do the best we can with what we have through knowledge and relationships with other parents and never forget the wisdom from our own parents. If they are no longer with you, find an aunt or uncle that you trust. Sit with them and draw wisdom from them. It is imperative to let our daughters know they are loved, for, from this love, comes correction. Mom and dad, be available for her and let her know you are there for her.

Final Words

Whether both parents are in the home or not, each parent needs to make time for their children, be they boys or girls. My suggestion to you is to make and take the time to bond with your children. Now, back to the daughters…

Mom, there should be one day each month, week, or every other week in which you spend time with your daughter. You don't have to always go out; you can do things at home. For instance, watch a movie, make a meal, play a board game, or even exercise together.

Dad, you can do the same thing, but, if you haven't been in the picture for a while, I would suggest you go to her favorite restaurant, break bread, get to know each other. Share your youth experiences, talk about grandparents, aunts, uncles, and cousins she might not know about.

Remarried? Slowly bring the other siblings and wife into the picture. A blended family can work, but it takes hard work. There may be bumps along the way, but don't give up! Remember: your first daughter is just as important as your second or third. Pray and ask God for guidance or do family counseling. This may help set the tone in a positive direction. Never compare the siblings; let them know that kind of behavior will not be tolerated. Mom, do not discourage this process because you are a big part of this, too!

*****

My prayer is that everyone who reads this book will become encourage and willing to take another try at having a relationship with their daughter. They will also allow God to heal all hurts and wounds of the past so there can be positive forward movement. Never forget that God loves you; God is always with you; and He hears your prayers.

Go ahead, take the first step…. It's worth it.

48

Brenda Miller

Bibliography

Lang, Gregory E. *Why a Daughter Needs a Dad: 100 Reasons*. Naperville: Cumberland House, 2004, 2012.

Lang, Gregory E. *Why a Daughter Needs a Mom: 100 Reasons*. Nashville: Cumberland House, 2004